THE **REAL** Story:
DEBUNKING HISTORY

THE REAL STORY BEHIND THE

CIVIL WAR

LISA IDZIKOWSKI

PowerKiDS
press

New York

Published in 2020 by The Rosen Publishing Group, Inc.
29 East 21st Street, New York, NY 10010

First Edition

Editor: Jill Keppeler
Book Design: Reann Nye

Photo Credits: Cover De Agostini Picture Library/Getty Images; p. 5 Rainer Lesniewski/Shutterstock.com; p. 7 (top) https://commons.wikimedia.org/wiki/File:Abraham_lincoln_inauguration_1861.jpg; p. 7 (bottom) https://commons.wikimedia.org/wiki/File:Abraham_Lincoln_O-55,_1861-crop.jpg; p. 8 https://commons.wikimedia.org/wiki/File:Alexander_Stephens.jpg; p. 9 https://commons.wikimedia.org/wiki/File:Detroit_Photographic_Company_(0780).jpg; p. 11 UniversalImagesGroup/Universal Images Group/Getty Images; p. 13 Historical/Corbis Historical/Getty Images; pp. 15, 17, 21 (bottom), 23 (bottom), 25 Courtesy of the Library of Congress; p. 16 https://commons.wikimedia.org/wiki/File:George_Peter_Alexander_Healy_-_John_C._Calhoun_-_Google_Art_Project.jpg; p. 19 John Parrot/Stocktrek Images/Getty Images; p. 21 (top) Buyenlarge/Archive Photos/Getty Images; p. 23 (top) Archive Photos/Getty Images; p. 26 https://commons.wikimedia.org/wiki/File:John_Wilkes_Booth_CDV_by_Black_%26_Case.jpg; p. 27 (Lee) https://commons.wikimedia.org/wiki/File:Robert_Edward_Lee.jpg; P. 27 (Grant) https://en.wikipedia.org/wiki/File:Ulysses_S._Grant_1870-1880.jpg; p. 27 (bottom) Universal History Archive/Universal Images Group/Getty Images; p. 28 KAREN BLEIER/AFP/Getty Images; p. 29 WilliamSherman/Getty Images.

Library of Congress Cataloging-in-Publication Data

Names: Idzikowski, Lisa, author.
Title: The real story behind the Civil War / Lisa Idzikowski.
Description: New York : PowerKids Press, [2020] | Series: The real story : debunking history | Includes index.
Identifiers: LCCN 2018031082| ISBN 9781538343449 (library bound) | ISBN 9781538344644 (pbk.) | ISBN 9781538344651 (6 pack)
Subjects: LCSH: United States–History–Civil War, 1861-1865–Juvenile literature.
Classification: LCC E468 .I39 2010 | DDC 973.7–dc23
LC record available at https://lccn.loc.gov/2018031082

Manufactured in the United States of America

CPSIA Compliance Information: Batch #CSPK19. For Further Information contact Rosen Publishing, New York, New York at 1-800-237-9932

CONTENTS

LIBERTY AND THE CIVIL WAR

Many Americans believe in the words of the Declaration of Independence. But liberty, as in "life, liberty, and the pursuit of happiness," means different things to different people. In the 1800s in particular, many people in the North and South held opposing ideas. Misunderstandings, mistrust, and resentment were common. Once united in their fight against the British during the Revolutionary War, Americans began seeing each other as enemies. By 1861, these differences exploded in the American Civil War.

It's vital to learn about and from the Civil War period. By digging down through layers of misinformation, made-up tales, and repeated misunderstandings, we come closer to the truth about our nation's history.

NORTH AGAINST SOUTH

The U.S. Civil War was a fierce conflict between the states. Twenty-three states in the northern and western parts of the country remained in the Union. These states supported the federal government. Eleven states in the south of the country seceded from, or left, the Union. They formed their own government and were known as the Confederate States of America.

FACT FINDER

The American Civil War is also known as the War Between the States, the War of the **Rebellion**, and, in the South, the War of Northern **Aggression**.

MINNESOTA

WISCONSIN

MICHIGAN

IOWA

ILLINOIS INDIANA OHIO

KANSAS

MISSOURI KENTUCKY

TENNESSEE

ARKANSAS

MISSISSIPPI ALABAMA GEORGIA

TEXAS

LOUISIANA

FLORIDA

SOUTH
CAROLINA

NORTH
CAROLINA

WEST
VIRGINIA VIRGINIA

PENNSYLVANIA

NEW YORK

NEW HAMPSHIRE
VERMONT
MAINE

MASSACHUSETTS
RHODE ISLAND
CONNECTICUT
NEW JERSEY
DELAWARE
MARYLAND

UNION STATES WITHOUT SLAVES

UNION STATES WITH SLAVES

CONFEDERATE STATES

5

WHY THE NORTH FOUGHT

Why did the North go to war with the South? To end slavery is usually the first thing people think of, but this isn't entirely true. In the beginning, the North didn't go to war because of slavery in the South. Most Northerners, including Abraham Lincoln, believed in preserving the Union. They wished to keep the United States together as one nation.

In his speech after being sworn in as president, Abraham Lincoln said he had no plan "to interfere with the institution of slavery in the States where it exists." With these words, Lincoln was trying to calm the worries of Southerners. His first goal was to keep as many states as possible from leaving the Union.

LINCOLN CHANGES HIS GOAL

Abraham Lincoln didn't like slavery. He once said, "If slavery is not wrong, nothing is wrong." In addition to keeping the United States together as one nation, he also felt a duty to stop the spread of slavery to newly formed states. Months after the Civil War began, President Lincoln began figuring out how to accomplish these goals. He needed to win the war. And to do that, the **abolition** of slavery was key.

FACT FINDER

When Abraham Lincoln spoke to the nation at his first inaugural address on March 4, 1861, seven states had already seceded from the Union.

Crowds surround the U.S. Capitol on the day of Abraham Lincoln's first inauguration, or swearing in, as president.

ABRAHAM LINCOLN

ACCORDING TO THE SOUTH

Southerners had different reasons for seceding and for fighting in the Civil War. States' rights are one reason often given for the war, but slavery was the root of the conflict. Many of the Northern states had already abolished slavery, but many Southerners believed they needed slaves to maintain their agricultural economy and way of life.

On March 21, 1861, Alexander Stephens, the vice president of the new Confederate States of America, said that slavery was "the immediate cause" of the war. He went on to explain that the new Confederate government was based "upon the great truth that the [black man] is not equal to the white man" and that slavery is a "natural and normal condition."

ALEXANDER STEPHENS

FACT FINDER

On April 12, 1861, Confederate forces fired on Fort Sumter in South Carolina. This was the start of the Civil War.

Fort Sumter was on an island near Charleston, South Carolina. Today, the site of the fort is a national monument.

Secession may have set off the Civil War, but the Southern states seceded because of slavery. They were worried that Lincoln, if elected president, would find a way to end slavery.

Lincoln firmly believed that no state should be able to "lawfully get out of the Union." But shortly after he was elected president, South Carolina seceded. In their reasons, state leaders said their right to keep "property in slaves" was given by the U.S. Constitution and that the federal government was threatening that right. The state leaders also argued that non-slaveholding states had an increasing **hostility** to slavery and charged President Lincoln with being "hostile to slavery."

SOME SOUTHERN STATES STAYED

Not all states in the South seceded. Border states Kentucky, Missouri, Maryland, and Delaware remained loyal to the Union, even though all four still permitted slavery as the war began. They were very important to the Union war effort. President Lincoln did all he could to keep them on the Union side. Some parts of Virginia also stayed loyal to the Union. They eventually split off into the state of West Virginia.

FACT FINDER

On December 20, 1860, South Carolina became the first state to secede from the Union.

In 1860, South Carolina had about 402,000 of the almost 4 million slaves in the United States.

DID EVERYONE OWN SLAVES?

It might seem that everyone in the South owned slaves. Otherwise, why would they support slavery enough to secede and fight in a war against the Union? But this was definitely not true. Information from the 1860 United States **Census** shows this.

At the time of the census, nearly 31 million people lived in the United States. Almost 4 million of these people were slaves. Of the 36 states and territories at that time, 19 reported no slaves. Kansas (which became a state in January 1861) reported two slaves. Nebraska, which was still a territory, reported 15 slaves. However, five states (Alabama, Georgia, Mississippi, South Carolina, and Virginia) had more than 400,000 slaves each. Virginia alone had nearly 500,000 enslaved people. Still, only 8 percent of U.S. families owned slaves.

SO WHY DID THEY FIGHT?

So, if only a relatively small percentage of the people of the South owned the greatest number of slaves, why did so many people fight to protect slavery? The great slave owners convinced the smaller farmers that slavery was important to their way of life. And even if the smaller farmers didn't own slaves, they hoped to do so someday. They also were frightened by the idea that the great numbers of slaves could be free and living as their equals.

FACT FINDER

In 1860, nearly 50 percent of families living in Mississippi and South Carolina owned slaves.

12

Only a small number of Southerners owned the large plantations on which many African Americans were enslaved. This picture shows an idealized plantation without the awful conditions many slaves endured.

SLAVE OR SERVANT?

One lasting myth is that Africans and African Americans weren't the only enslaved people in the United States. Some people say that Irish Americans were held as slaves, too. Some Southerners used this story to argue that the North had slaves.

It's true that many Irish immigrants came to the United States as **indentured servants**. And it's true that Irish workers were sometimes called "Irish slaves." But indentured servants only worked as such for a set amount of time. According to a written contract, they would be free from indenture at some time in their future.

Unlike indentured servants, slaves almost never stopped being slaves. Children born to indentured servants were free. Children born to an enslaved mother were also slaves and the property of their mother's owner.

FACT FINDER

Indentured servants worked under contracts that commonly lasted for two to seven years.

This photo represents five generations of a slave family. Any children born to slaves were slaves themselves.

"A POSITIVE GOOD"

It's shocking today that people could consider slavery a good thing. But some did—or at least said they did. In the 1820s and 1830s, some people, especially Southern whites, described slavery as a "positive good."

This was in part due to the debates over the statehood of Missouri, starting in 1820. Politicians from the North and South fought fiercely over whether the new state would allow slavery. Southerners began to justify slavery as a good thing for both plantation owners and slaves alike. Slave owners, they said, needed slaves to work on the plantations, growing and harvesting cotton. They said the slaves benefited by being cared for by their owners and having the exposure to white "civilization." Today, arguments to justify slavery sound unbelievable, but some people did believe them.

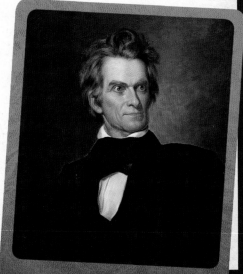

JOHN C. CALHOUN

In 1837, politician John C. Calhoun of South Carolina used the words "a positive good" when referring to slavery in a speech. He later became a U.S. senator and secretary of state.

THE PROCLAMATIONS

On September 22, 1862, President Abraham Lincoln issued the **Emancipation Proclamation**, which was to take effect January 1, 1863. Unless Confederate forces stopped fighting and rejoined the Union, Lincoln's proclamation announced, "all persons held as slaves" in the rebelling states "shall be then, thenceforward, and forever free." Many people take this to mean it ended slavery. Did it?

No. January 1, 1863, came and went, and most slaves in the Union and Confederacy were unaffected. Not only did the proclamation only apply to the states that were rebelling—and not the ones that were already under Union control or part of the Union—but Southern slave owners certainly weren't going to free their slaves on Lincoln's command. The Union would have to win the war for Lincoln's words to mean more.

A CHANGED WAR

It may not have ended slavery, but the Emancipation Proclamation was important because it changed the stated goals of the war. Up to this point, Lincoln had maintained that the Civil War was being fought to keep the country together. The proclamation turned the Civil War into a fight to end slavery. As the Union army advanced, many slaves took their freedom. Some joined the army. This also weakened the Confederacy.

FACT FINDER

The 13th Amendment, which ended slavery, was ratified, or approved, by the states on December 6, 1865.

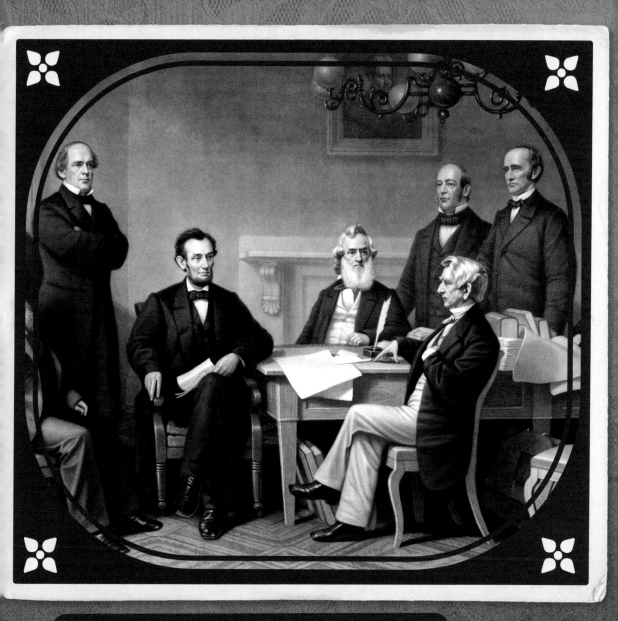

This painting shows Abraham Lincoln about to read the Emancipation Proclamation to the members of his cabinet in July 1862.

FIGHTING FOR THE CONFEDERACY?

One persistent Civil War myth is that many African Americans (free and slaves) fought for the Confederacy, even though the Confederacy was trying to protect slavery. There is no question that many black people were on the front lines, but white Confederate officers usually had brought them as slaves. They cooked, washed clothes, assisted in hospitals, and labored at other tasks without a choice.

In fact, Confederate President Jefferson Davis refused to even discuss the idea of African Americans as soldiers—at least, not until the end of the war. Starting in March 1865, the Confederate army did allow black men to join as soldiers, but their owners had to free them first, so there weren't many.

CONTRABAND OF WAR

In May 1861, three slaves fled their Confederate work camp and escaped across a river to a Union outpost in Virginia. A Confederate officer tried to recover the escapees, but Union General Benjamin Butler refused to hand the men over. Instead, Butler said he would keep the men "as contraband of war." Soon, "contraband of war" came to mean a former slave who'd escaped to the Union.

FACT FINDER

About 200,000 African American men had fought in the Union army by the end of the Civil War.

20

After escaping, many African American "contrabands" were ready to work for the Union.

<

DEATH, DISEASE, AND DOCTORS

The Civil War was a very bloody, deadly war. Given all the battles and violence, it's easy to suppose that all or most soldier deaths were in battle. However, disease and **infection** caused two-thirds of the deaths in the Civil War.

Many people have an image of Civil War medicine as primitive and dirty, with many soldiers enduring unnecessary **amputations** with no **anesthesia**. However, while amputations were common and doctors didn't clearly understand germs yet, the conditions weren't quite that bad. Doctors worked hard to save lives, and in many cases, amputating a limb was more likely to save a life than trying to save the limb. Various kinds of anesthesia were used to help keep soldiers from suffering.

WHAT'S A GERM?

At the time of the Civil War, many people didn't understand the role, or part, that germs played in disease. Many thought "bad air" filled with poisons or gases caused disease and death. Today, we understand that germs—bacteria and viruses—cause health problems. Doctors can give people antibiotics that help them fight off infections and disease.

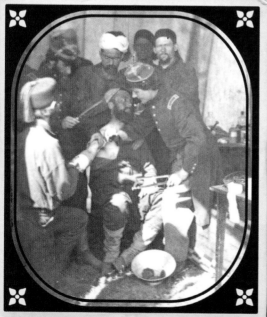

Above, members of the
Union ambulance corps
load injured soldiers
into a horse-drawn
wagon for transport to
a hospital. During the
Civil War, hospitals
gained a better
reputation than they
had before the war.

SO MANY DEATHS

We know that many people were injured or died in the Civil War, but it's difficult to get a clear number. Different experts give different estimates of the deaths and other casualties, or those who were killed or lost from battle due to disease, capture, or injury. This is due to a lack of clear records, the large number of soldiers who were hurt or killed, and the overall chaos caused by the war.

In 1889, two Civil War veterans studying army records calculated that about 620,000 deaths occurred—or roughly 2 percent of the total U.S. population. In more recent years, researchers have estimated that up to 850,000 people died due to the war. Experts still disagree about this.

FACT FINDER

The deadliest battle of the Civil War occurred at Gettysburg, Pennsylvania, where there were about 51,000 casualties.

This oil painting shows a scene from the battle of Gettysburg.

END OF THE WAR

It's commonly accepted that the Civil War ended when the Army of Northern Virginia under General Robert E. Lee surrendered to General Ulysses S. Grant on April 9, 1865, at Appomattox Court House, Virginia. However, while this was the beginning of the end, fighting continued.

The Army of Tennessee (which included about 90,000 men) didn't surrender until April 26, 1865. Union forces captured Confederate president Jefferson Davis on May 10, 1865, and the final battle of the war took place May 13, 1865, at Palmito Ranch, Texas. This battle was a Confederate victory, but two weeks later, the Confederate army surrendered. The long war was finally over.

Abraham Lincoln didn't live to see the end, however. He died April 14, 1865, killed by John Wilkes Booth in Washington, D.C.

JOHN WILKES BOOTH

ULYSSES S. GRANT

ROBERT E. LEE

General Robert E. Lee surrenders to General Ulysses S. Grant at Appomattox Court House.

27

A JUST WAR?

Was the Civil War a just war? If a just war begins because of self-defense, you could make a case that the North was defending the Union from the South, starting with the attack on Fort Sumter. However, Fort Sumter is in South Carolina and thus in the Confederacy itself. Some people think the Confederate states had a right to secede if they wanted to. However, in 1869, the U.S. Supreme Court ruled that states do not have that right.

You can also justify the war by saying that it ended slavery, so it must have been just. However, the North didn't start out by fighting to end slavery, although the South fought to keep it. People still disagree about the Civil War today. Perhaps they always will.

People take part in Civil War reenactments even today. This one is taking place July 4, 2013, in Gettysburg, Pennsylvania.

A COMPLEX WAR

The Civil War is a **complex** subject, and many people still feel strongly about it. Because of that, more than 150 years after the first shots were fired, there are still many chances for misunderstandings, misinformation, and disagreements.

In both the North and the South, people believed they were fighting for their homes and their **heritage**. It can be hard to face the reasons for the war and the echoes of violence and slavery that still exist today. But if we look through the stories and the myths, we can start to understand the roots of the war and the conflicts that came before it and after it. If we learn from the past, we will be better prepared not to repeat its mistakes in the future.

GLOSSARY

abolition: The act of officially ending or stopping something, especially slavery.

aggression: Showing a readiness to attack.

amputation: The act of cutting off an arm or leg from the body.

anesthesia: Loss of feeling in the body or part of the body, often due to drugs meant to help during medical operations.

census: The official process of counting the number of people in a country or an area.

complex: Not easy to understand or explain; having many parts.

contraband: Something brought into or out of a country illegally.

Emancipation Proclamation: The piece of writing issued by Lincoln that said slaves in Confederate states were free.

heritage: The traditions and beliefs that are part of the history of a group or nation.

hostility: An unfriendly attitude or action.

indentured servant: A person who is bound to work for another for a specific period of time, often in exchange for passage to a new country.

infection: A sickness caused by germs entering the body.

rebellion: Open fighting against authority.

INDEX

WEBSITES

Due to the changing nature of Internet links, PowerKids Press has developed an online list of websites related to the subject of this book. This site is updated regularly. Please use this link to access the list: www.powerkidslinks.com/debunk/civil